4862
Rock Climbing (Action Sports Library)

Bob Italia
AR B.L.: 6.5
Points: 1.0                    MG

*Action Sports Library*

# Rock Climbing

**Bob Italia**

Published by Abdo & Daughters, 4940 Viking Drive, Suite 622, Edina, Minnesota 55435.

Library bound edition distributed by Rockbottom Books, Pentagon Tower, P.O. Box 36036, Minneapolis, Minnesota 55435.

Printed in the United States.

Cover Photo credit: Adventure Photo
Interior Photo credits: Adventure Photo—4, 13, 27
Westlight—9, 10, 15, 19, 22, 28

**Illustrations by Kristen Copham**
**Edited by Kal Gronvall**

> **Warning:** The series *Action Sports Library* is intended as entertainment for children.  These sporting activities should never be attempted without proper conditioning, training, instruction, supervision, and equipment.

## Library of Congress Cataloging-in-Publication Data

Italia, Bob, 1955-
    Rock climbing / Bob Italia
    p.  cm. -- (Action sports library)
    Includes bibliographical references.
    ISBN 1-56239-342-1
    1. Rock climbing--Juvenile literature. [1. Rock climbing.]
    I. Title. II Series: Italia, Bob, 1955- Action sports library.
    GV200.2.I83  1994
    796.5'223--dc20
                                            94-12496
                                                CIP
                                                  AC

# Contents

## A Breathtaking Sport

Rock climbing is not a new sport.  But these days, it has taken on a new luster.  Where ever you see a challenging wall of rock, chances are you'll find a team of climbers attempting to scale it. Some schools even offer rock climbing as a class, and have gymnasium walls specially designed for climbing practice.

The lure of rock climbing is not a mystery.  It is challenging, fun, and exciting.  With the proper help and training, anyone can enjoy this breathtaking sport.

## Where Do You Start?

One way to learn rock climbing is to find a friend and work out climbing techniques of your own. You can also try to learn from a book. A climbing book will teach you about climbing.  But climbing skills cannot be learned solely from a book. The best way to learn climbing is with experienced climbers.

The first thing to do is to find knowledgeable climbers who will help you learn.  One of the best ways to find these people is to gather around climbers in popular climbing areas. Climbing schools are also available in many communities. Some high schools and colleges offer climbing and mountaineering courses. Professional guides can also be hired near major climbing areas.

One way is to locate a climbing club in a school or in a popular rock climbing geographical region. Some rock climbing clubs specialize in climbing only.  Some are general outdoor groups that sponsor hikes, ski trips, conservation activities, and mountaineering.

Each club has its own regulations and methods.  But almost all offer opportunities for beginners to learn. An important advantage of a club is that dedicated members are available as companions as you scale the heights together on your way to becoming a skilled climber.

## Learning to Climb

Beginning climbers should start their first climb in a place where large boulders or low cliffs provide a good practice area. Here you will learn the basic techniques of safe climbing.

Wear rubber-soled shoes and old clothes suitable for the weather. The members of the rock climbing club or the instructor usually brings the climbing equipment. Beginners must use the ropes at all times. Always treat climbing ropes with care. Never step on them, pull them through the dirt, or drag them over sharp edges.

## Knots

Remember, your rope is your only protection. So, you must learn to tie foolproof knots that are and easy to tie and untie. Choosing a proper knot will depend mainly on group or individual preference.

Practice tying your knots with a piece of rope or cord until you can tie them expertly under any condition. Individual knots may have several names. The most common are described below.

### Bowline

The bowline is a knot used for fastening the end of the rope around your waist. First, pass the rope behind you from left to right. Next, hold the long or "standing" part of the rope in your left hand, and the short end in your right hand. Then with the left hand, make a loop. Doubling this loop will add about five percent to the strength of the knot. Finally, put the other end up through the loop, around the standing end, and back down through the loop.

After tying the knot, work the loop along the rope until the waist loop is really snug. Test the knot and set with a good tug. The bowline knot tends to loosen with use. So safeguarded it by tying one or two overhand knots around the waist loop. Several inches of rope should be left over after the knot is secured. During a climb, check the bowline occasionally, and tighten the waist loop if necessary.

### Bowline-on-a-Coil

The bowline-on-a-coil is a knot that is useful in the event of a fall. It will help absorb the shock. To tie this knot, wind the rope around your waist several times. Tie the knot around the coil. Now hold onto the short end and jerk the standing end to complete the knot. Test it and secure with overhands.

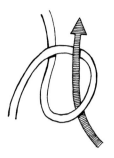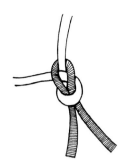

*THE BOWLINE*

*BOWLINE-ON-A-COIL*

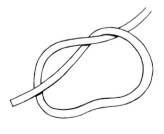

*OVERHAND*

### Water Knot or Ring Bend

The water knot or ring bend is used to join the ends of flat nylon webbing or light rope to form slings. First, tie an overhand knot loosely in one end, and thread the other end through it in the opposite direction. Next, with the flat nylon webbing, make sure the two parts of the knot lie flat against each other throughout. Set the knot hard, and secure each end with an overhand knot.

### Figure Eight Loop

The figure eight loop is a knot that is used to tie into the middle of a rope. First, tie a figure eight knot in a doubled section (see illustration). Be sure to leave a loop large enough to slip over your head and arms. Adjust this loop to a snug fit around your waist by sliding the knot along the rope.

### Flemish Bend or Figure Eight Bend

The Flemish bend or figure eight bend is a knot that is used to join two ropes of the same or unequal diameters. This knot resembles the water knot, but is much easier to untie when set. First, start by tying a loose figure eight knot in one of the rope ends. Be sure to allow several extra inches for a safety knot. Next, thread one end of the second rope through the knot in the opposite direction. Make sure that the two ropes lie parallel to each other throughout the knot. Then, tighten and test by pulling hard in opposite directions on the standing ends of the two ropes. This is especially important if the ropes are of unequal diameters. The thinner rope tends to slip out of an improperly formed knot. Finally, secure the knot on each side with one or more overhand knots.

### Prussik

The prussik is a knot that is an essential aid if, in an emergency, you must climb a rope. The average person is unable to climb a long rope hand over hand. And ascending your climbing rope in this way would allow slack to develop and deprive you of protection.

Prussik knots are formed by twisting slings around a rope that is anchored above you. The climber stands in these loops, which remain in place when weighted but can be slipped up or down when unweighted. The slings should be approximately five or six feet in circumference. They will vary in size to fit the person and to allow the knots to be in front of the chest for easy handling.

*WATER KNOT*

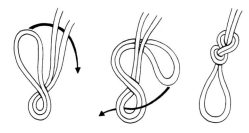

*FIGURE EIGHT LOOP*

 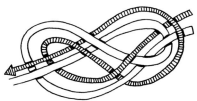 

*FLEMISH BEND*

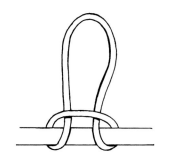 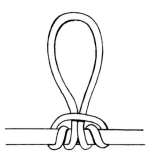 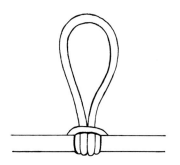

*PRUSSIK*

A standard technique for ascending a rope with prussiks is to use three slings attached at intervals to the vertical rope. One loop is a chest loop (for balance) and the other two loops are for footsteps. The chest loop goes over the head and the arms. One foot loop should be longer than the other. Balance is improved by tying the slings into smaller loops with a figure eight knot, forming stirrups for the feet. For convenience and versatility, the two lower prussiks may be tied using short slings, with *etriers* (ladderlike slings) clipped into them.

To ascend, stand with all your weight in the lowest sling. Now raise the next sling as high as you can step. Transfer your weight to the upper footstep. Raise the chest loop as high as you can for balance. Pull up the rope hanging below you so you can reach the lower foot loop. Slip this loop up as far as possible, using both hands. Stand in it so you can raise the upper foot loop. Repeat this sequence, and up you go! At first, it is difficult and tiring. But it gets easier with practice.

## Climbing With the Rope

Once tied in, you can begin your climb. Have someone on the rocks above belaying you in case of a fall. Remember, the rope is only a protective device, not a handhold.

The climber's legs normally do most of the work. The hands and arms function to provide balance and some pull. Try not to use your knees. This makes climbing awkward.

The key to an effortless ascent is balance. To maintain balance, remember to keep your body weight over your feet and away from the rock in front of you at exactly the right angle to make full use of whatever support the holds provide. Balance is increased by use of momentum. It enables you to glide up the rocks instead of struggling.

### Climbing Moves

Friction between the sole of your boot and the rock in front of you that keeps you from slipping. The first climbing move is called momentum. Momentum allows progress where you cannot stand still. The second move is called the mantel. A mantel is when you push yourself up on a ledge with the heel of your hand.

The third move is called chimneying. Chimneying involves the use of various counter-pressures of the back, arms, knees, and feet against opposing rock walls. Chimneying allows you to wiggle upwards without real holds.

Other moves use various types of hand or foot jams in suitable cracks. And there's the lieback or layback, a move where feet walk up the face of a cliff while your hands and arms pull in the opposite direction to create enough pressure to keep your feet from slipping.

### Upper Belays

Your rope has two purposes. It gets you where you are going, and it also protects you. An important step for participating in roped climbing is acquiring the knowledge and skill to also protect other climbers. Giving an upper belay to someone climbing below you is an introduction to protecting a climber.

To give an upper belay, sit down in a safe spot, feet apart and firmly braced. You should face the climber and be tied to a rock, tree, piton, or chocks so you cannot possibly be pulled off. Pass the rope coming up from the climber below around your hips. Next, hold the rope with both hands, one hand on each side of your body.

*Giving an upper belay to a fellow climber.*

The hand on the climber's end guides, feels, and takes in the rope as the climber ascends. The other hand holds the weight in case of a fall. The friction of the rope around your hips makes both of these things easy to do.

Take in the rope by moving the "feeling" hand toward the body. At the same time extend the belay hand away from the body, pulling the rope with it. Quickly slide both hands along the rope to their former positions.

Your belay hand must never let go of the rope. If you have trouble sliding it along the slack rope, the "feeling" hand can grasp the belaying part of the rope. Grab it between your thumb and fingertips to provide a little tension. Once you have control again, continue to take in rope.

While you are learning to belay, the climber below should call "Testing!" before he starts to climb. Reply "Test!" and he will give a gradual but strong pull so you can get an idea of how it might feel if he or she fell off.

### Handling the Rope

While belaying, you must watch the rope carefully. Lay the rope you pull up in a pile and put it in a place where it is unlikely to snag on anything or knock off rocks. Keep the rope just tight enough so you can feel the climber, but don't pull. Your guiding hand tells you how fast to take in the rope.

The person climbing also has another important responsibility. He or she must keep the rope free of kinks, must notice if it snags or catches, and must make sure the climber does not overclimb the rope. If slack develops, he or she should slow down or stop until the rope is again taut.

### Climbing Signals

Climbers on the same rope are frequently out of each other's sight and may not be able to hear each other. Yet it is important that each knows what the other is doing. A set of verbal signals has been standardized among climbers:

Belayer: "Belay on!"
Climber: "Climbing!"
Belayer: "Climb!"

When climber wants the belayer to take in more rope, or to take it in faster: "Rope!" or "'Up rope!"

When climber wants the belayer to support him or her on the rope: "Tension!"

When climber needs less tension, or extra slack for maneuvering, descending, throwing the rope, etc.: "Slack!"

Climber, to warn belayer, "Prepare for fall!" or "Falling!"

Or, if a rock (or other object) falls: "Rock!"

When climber is in a safe position near the belayer (or elsewhere): "Belay off!"

Belayer: "Belay off!"

"Rope" and "Slack" signals are usually repeated by the person for whom they are meant.  These calls are repeated as a confirmation that he or she has heard, understood, and is taking appropriate action.  Even moderate winds can make it impossible to hear shouts.  As a result, you may have to shout as loudly as you can.  But do not assume that the other climber has heard the signal until you get an answer.

In addition to the winds hindering your hearing, steep rocks often keep the climbers from seeing each other.  So, you will have to develop different ways to communicate with the other climbers.  For instance, varying numbers of tugs on the rope can transmit signals, but tugs are not always foolproof.

### Learning to Rappel

Climbers have developed several methods of descending steep rocks by sliding down a rope which has been doubled around a fixed point. These methods are called "rappelling," or "roping down."

To rappel, begin with a simple body rappel with a belay for safety. This basic rappel is generally modified for long descents. Every rock climber should know about rappelling because the only equipment required is the rope.

To get into the rappel, stand below the point around which the rope is doubled. Face the cliff and straddle the doubled rope. Take hold of the doubled rope behind you, and bring it forward across the left hip. Pull it up across your chest, and backwards over your right shoulder. The doubled rope now hangs down behind you. Grasp the rope with your left (lower) hand, palm forward and thumb downward.  The lower hand supports your weight and holds you into the rope. So, you must never let it go. The right (upper) hand holds on to the rope above you for balance, and is the one to be used for any necessary adjustments. A left-handed person may prefer to reverse the arrangement.

Once in the rope, lean backwards. Your body should be at about a forty-five-degree angle to the rock. Your knees should be bent slightly and your feet should be twenty-four to thirty-six inches apart for balance on the varying inclines. Look down frequently over your left shoulder to see where you are going. Then walk backwards or sideways down the cliff. The rope will slide slowly through your hands and over your body.

The points of greatest friction are where the rope passes over your hip and shoulder. They become very hot if you go too fast. Extra padding is recommended at these points. Your lower hand controls the speed of your descent. It is important to remember that nothing is gained by gripping the rope frantically with the upper hand. Once at the bottom of your descent, make sure your footing is good, and step out of the rope. Call "Off rappel!" to those above.

### Coiling the Rope

One of the beginner's duties is to learn how to coil the climbing rope for carrying and storage. A popular coiling method is called the Mountaineer's Coil. It is quick and easy to coil and uncoil. With one hand, gather up successive coils about five feet in circumference and place them neatly in the other hand. Don't fight the rope if it twists into a figure eight. Just leave it that way.

Bend the starting end of the rope back on itself for a foot or so and keep this loop secure with your holding hand. Wrap the last few feet of the other end of the rope closely and firmly around the coils where they are held together. Pass the end of the rope through the loop. Then pull both ends tight, and tie a square knot for extra protection.

## Climbing Equipment

Soon after you start climbing, you will need some personal equipment. Such equipment varies according to geographical area and according to the people with whom you climb. Observe what equipment your companions are using and ask their advice. Go slow about buying equipment until you know what you really want and need. Many sporting goods stores handle or specialize in mountaineering supplies. There are also excellent mail-order sources which publish informative catalogs. If you become seriously interested in rock climbing, you should gradually acquire some or all of the equipment discussed in this book.

### Rock Climbing Shoes

Specialized shoes are a basic requirement for all serious rock climbers. While heavy boots are a must for mixed rock and snow climbing, rock shoes are much better for serious rock work. The best styles have high-friction rubber soles. These shoes have rubber extending up the toes, heels, and sides for greater gripping power in jam cracks and also for reinforcement. These shoes should fit snugly over one pair of light socks. A tight fit aids edging, but shoes that are too snug become painful for walking.

*A harness makes climbing easier and safer.*

### Harness

Tying the rope around your waist is adequate for practice climbing while belayed from above. But a seat harness provides far greater safety and convenience in real ascents than does simply tying the rope around your waist. The addition of a chest harness to the seat harness increases safety, especially if you hang awhile. Tie the rope to the seat harness with a bowline, preferably doubled.

### Swami Belt

Some climbers wear a fifteen-foot length of one-inch nylon webbing wound around their waist and secured snugly with a water knot.

A better and safer arrangement is to make what climbers call a swami belt. To make a swami belt, first make leg loops in the webbing to keep the waist loop from riding up around your in case you fall. Use one-inch webbing about 25 feet long. Tie two leg loops that fit at crotch level, using an overhand knot. One loop should be about five feet from the end of the webbing, the other loop should be six or seven inches from the short end.

Put your right leg through the loop that is closest to the short end of the webbing, and your left leg through the other loop. Pull the loops up to your crotch. Run the long end of the webbing counterclockwise around your back, through the left loop, around your back again, and through the right-hand leg loop. Then wind both ends of the webbing around your waist as many times as the length permits. Tie the ends together with a water knot, and secure them with overhand knots. Attach the climbing rope to the swami in the same way as to a harness.

### Climbing Rope

The climbing rope must be of synthetic material (nylon or perlon) for strength and elasticity. It should also be manufactured especially for mountaineering. There are two main types: laid (twisted) or sheath (kernmantle) construction. A hard-lay nylon rope serves well for a beginning or occasional climber. Its advantages are lower cost and ease of inspection for damage. However, it can be stiff and has a tendency to kink.

A kernmantle rope of perlon has a core of continuous filaments which provide strength. It also has a woven sheath to protect the core. It is lighter in weight, and seasoned rock climbers prefer it for long serious rock climbs. They prefer the perlon rope because it creates less rope drag than a laid rope.

Most climbers use kernmantle rope 150 feet in length for rock climbs. Climbers using laid rope generally select 7/16 inch diameter rope 150 feet long. Shorter ropes are convenient and save weight on high peaks and glaciers. "Big wall" climbs have few belay points. So, climbers prefer 165-foot lengths.

### Slings or Runners

Slings, also called runners, are loops used for different types of protection and for varied purposes. They may be ready-made or constructed from flat nylon webbing, usually one inch wide, or from perlon rope. These slings vary from about three to eight feet in circumference after the knot is tied. Longer slings can be formed quickly by joining two or more slings together. All perlon and nylon sling material, when cut, should immediately have the ends fused with flame to prevent raveling. After the ends are fused, tie the ends together with a water knot, set hard, and secure with overhand knots. Always carry several assorted slings with you.

Most climbers use a sling for carrying hardware. Instead of being knotted, this sling can have the ends overlapped and sewn together with strong thread. The lack of a knot is comfortable, and lets the hardware slide freely. Never use this sewn sling, however, for any other purpose as it may not be strong enough.

### Carabiners

Carabiners are snaplinks of aluminum alloy, usually oval or roughly pear-shaped, and about four inches long. They have a spring gate opening on one side, sometimes with a screw lock.

Carabiners are used to connect the climbing rope with a sling, which in turn is attached to a rock, tree or chock, or with the eye of a piton. They also are used to carry hardware or rig slings. Keep carabiners free of dust and grit, and never oil them because oil collects grime.

### Chocks or Nuts

Artificial chock stones—usually aluminum alloy—come in various shapes and sizes. They are used to wedge or jam into cracks for protection in difficult climbing, or to be used in difficult moves. They are threaded with slings of nylon webbing, perlon rope, or wire cable.

### Chock Picks

Chock picks are a must for removing chocks. Manufactured picks are the best.

### Helmets and Hats

Due to the number of head injuries in climbing (both from falling rock and from injuries sustained in leader falls), most seasoned rock climbers use hard hats or helmets. Rock climbing hard hats or helmets are sold in mountaineering shops. Important features of a good helmet include a good fit, a dependable and adjustable chin strap, the manufacturer's name, and information as to the strength under impact. Helmets weigh between one and one and a half pounds, and come in many colors.

If you don't want to or can't invest in a helmet, an ordinary felt hat is preferable to climbing bareheaded. It cushions your head from minor blows, shades you from sunburn, protects your glasses in the rain, and keeps dirt and sun out of your eyes. A felt hat also can be stuffed inside your shirt as insulation against rope burn in rappelling.

### Rucksack

A rucksack is a small summit pack, often of light tough nylon. It is needed to keep your gear together and to transport it to the start of the climb. It is also usually needed on the climb, and the least experienced member of the party, usually climbing third, may have the honor of carrying the party's supplies. So, the rucksack comes in handy for that purpose.

### Clothing

Temperatures are often far hotter or colder on the rocks than on the ground. The climate, the season of the year, possible stormy weather will often determine what clothing you will wear on a climb. Another thing that affects your choice of clothing is whether or not the climb will be in sun or in the shade. Don't forget the fabric-grinding effects of rock on clothes. Take extra boots and socks for long approaches. Rock shoes that are tight enough for climbing are often poor for hiking, particularly downhill. Pants should be loose enough so you can comfortably raise your foot to waist level.

### Other Equipment

A pocketknife, sunglasses, and sunburn lotion are also recommended. If you wear prescription glasses, secure them with a glasses strap so they can't fall off. A wristwatch may be damaged on a climb, so don't wear one.

As time goes by, ropes and slings wear out and eventually become unsafe. So, inspect them regularly for wear or damage. Replace them if you find signs of weakness.

## Climbing on Multi-Pitched Routes

Having practiced the basic techniques and having purchased some equipment, you are ready for multi-pitch climbing. A pitch is the distance climbed between belay spots, usually about 50 to 130 feet.

*Climbing routes are carefully selected before the climb begins.*

### Routes

Climbs are not made just anywhere on the cliff. A route usually goes up a portion of the cliff that has been broken by natural forces into connecting cracks, ledges, and chimneys. These natural connecting places offer handholds, footholds, niches for suitable chock or piton placement, and belay stances. Routes viewed from a distance may appear steep. A side view, however, usually reveals an easier angle for the route. Many times you will find more holds while actually climbing than there first appeared to be while you viewed the route from a distance. But the opposite may also be true, so be prepared.

### Climbing Parties

The word "rope" stands not only for the rope itself, but also stands for the climbing party that climbs tied together. The usual number of people on one rope is two or three. As a beginner, you will probably start consecutive climbing as third person at the end of the rope. As third person, you can learn what is involved with little responsibility, other than taking the responsibility for your own climbing. (The second person will protect both the leader and the third person.)

After the rope is made up, the climbers go to the foot of the route. Next, the climbers uncoil the climbing ropes and lay them in a loose pile (to prevent snarls). Finally, they adjust their hardware, and the climbers tie in.

### Order of Climbing

Every climb has a proper climbing order. For instance, the second climber takes the belay position, and the leader climbs. The leader may place protection occasionally. When he or she reaches the next belay spot, the leader stops, prepares to belay, and calls to the second to climb. You as third person are still waiting for the go-ahead.

When the second starts to climb, watch the rope going up to him or her. Make sure it does not snag. When the second person reaches the leader, he or she belays the leader up another pitch. You, the third climber, are again still waiting and watching. Be ready to climb as soon as the word comes down—and don't forget the rucksack.

When the leader is at the top of the second pitch, the second climber turns his or her attention to the third climber. If there is extra rope between you, he or she pulls it up. You should notify him or her when it is all up.

After you exchange signals, begin your climb. If you reach a chock or piton, you will see that the rope is running through a carabiner snapped into a sling or eye. Stop at a convenient place, remove the rope from the carabiner, remove the carabiner, and snap it into your waist loop or hardware rack. Call "Climbing!" to let your belayer know you are moving again.

When you reach the second climber, you will probably find he or she is anchored in with a sling or section of rope to a rock, tree, chocks, or piton. Tie yourself on in the same way. Hand the hardware you have collected to the second climber, who takes it along for the leader's use.

Be attentive to your ropemates' actions, needs, and instructions. Do not move until you receive the signal to climb. Watch and tend the rope. Once on the climb, it is a good idea for the third to belay the second. It gives practice in rope handling and is an extra safeguard for all. Remember to remove the anchor before starting the next pitch.

## Tips for Beginners

A few pointers may help on your first long climbs. Concentrate on the climbing. Watch the climbers ahead of you. It is very helpful to know which holds they use, and how, even though you may already know. Climb the pitch differently. Here is how. While climbing, look for holds, feel for them, try them with your hands and feet in different positions. Make all possible use of small holds close together to minimize the effort of hauling yourself up. Climb quickly. Many holds are fine for a swift smooth passage but not as a stopping place. Rest on large holds where you can relax.

You will probably be too busy to notice the empty spaces below, known as "exposure," or you may find it exhilarating. But if the empty spaces below bother you, look back at the rock and at the rope. You can then assure yourself that you are well-protected. Check your waist loop occasionally. Test handholds that might come off. If they are loose, find others. Be very careful not to dislodge rocks with your feet, hands, or with your rope.

If a rock does fall, yell "Rock! Rock!" for the benefit of anyone below. If you see or hear a rock coming from above, get your head up against the cliff, into a crack, or under an overhang—and be quick about it. If you cannot take cover, watch the rock and duck at the last second. Whenever possible, keep out from under climbers above.

Even if the climbing seems scarey and the chocks or pitons won't budge, don't complain. Ask the other climbers for advice, or make jokes—but don't say you can't! And don't talk too much. It distracts your companions and sometimes annoys them.

## Descending Multi-Pitched Climbs

Climbing up is only half the battle. Once you reach your destination, you have to climb down. There are two other modes of descent. Choose the one that is best for you.

### Walking Down

Walking down is usually the easiest and fastest, if a trail or easy terrain takes you where you want to go.

Granite walls make the best rock climbing routes.

*Climbing Down*

Climbing down is direct and quick on moderately easy climbs, either by the ascent route or by a different and easier known route. Descent by unknown climbing routes usually leads to trouble. Also, down climbing on purpose is a good way to gain experience before it is forced upon you.

Climbing down is often harder than going up the same rocks. That's because on the way down, It is hard to see the holds and the route. Face outwards as long as you can. When necessary, turn sideways.  At steep places where you must face the cliffs to use the holds, combine feeling with your feet and occasional inspections. In down climbing, the leader goes last to protect the party. The second climber should place protection below difficult moves.

## Where to Climb

Rock climbing is most popular in areas where accessible rock such as granite is adapted to the sport. In much-climbed areas, most routes are well established and have names. In non-mountainous areas, there may be bluffs, palisades, cliffs, ravines, boulders, quarries, and road cuts on which you can sharpen your techniques and have fun. Bouldering has also become a rock climbing specialty.

With or without good climbing nearby, you may want to travel to other places for some variety. With techniques and equipment to suit the place, you will find that every area has its own special appeal.

Extra care is needed on unfamiliar or unclimbed routes when you are a long way from help.   Climbing is also more difficult in heat, wind, and cold. Sudden changes in weather can change conditions from good to bad almost immediately. Even more, wet or snowy rocks are much more difficult and dangerous than dry ones.

Weather may also force you to retreat. Other reasons for giving up a climb include illness, fright, unwillingness, or injury in the party, unexpected route difficulties, and a shortage of equipment.

The most common reason for retreat is the lack of time to finish before dark. In deciding whether to go on or go back, remember that it may be quicker and safer to finish the climb if the top is closer than the bottom.  Continue the ascent only if you know that the climbing ahead is easier than the descent.

Roped climbing and rappelling in the dark are hazardous. If night overtakes you on the cliffs, it is usually best to tie on in a good place and stay put until daylight. When setting out next morning, adjust for the long hard night by using extra care.

Don't mess up the cliffs by leaving hardware or litter. A gum paper or juice can may seem unimportant to you when you drop them. But they will be offensive to the next fellow who comes across them. So don't litter.

When you become good at rock climbing, you will no longer be a beginner. You may well be on the way to becoming an expert rock climber if you continue climbing. Remember that rock climbing is only one branch of the complex sport of mountaineering, and you might not be ready for new challenges in new places and in new terrain.

## Safety Precautions on Trips

As a rock climber, the following additional safety precautions are valuable to help you keep out of trouble:

(I) Before each trip, leave word of your plans with someone who will notice and act if you don't return. Write down your plans and expected time of return. Add the name of a climbing friend, a ranger station, or a sheriff to notify if the need arises. Those at home should not panic if the party is a few hours or even a day overdue, as minor delays are often unavoidable.

(2) Have extra supplies in the car: water, food, spare clothing and shoes, and perhaps a blanket.

(3) Carry first aid supplies. Have a kit of your own, and be sure to carry one on your rope. It should contain an antiseptic, aspirins, adhesive tape, sterile gauze bandages and pads, a small pair of scissors, elastic bandage for sprains, and a splint—compact types can be inflatable or of hardware cloth. Waterproof matches, pencil, paper, and safety pins might be added.

(4) Pay attention to your surroundings.

(5) Use common sense as to weather, giving up a climb, etc.

(6) Prevent hypothermia. This condition, also known as "exposure," is the dangerous lowering of the body temperature. Hypothermia is caused by a combination of wet, cold, fatigue, and lack of food. The windchill factor is also especially important. Even a light wind can lower your body temperature, especially when your clothing is wet.

Hypothermia has been called "the killer of the unprepared." People carrying spare gear have died because they did not recognize the onset of the condition. They delayed putting on dry, warm clothing until they were so confused and chilled that it was impossible to recognize their own condition. Take spare clothes, and put the warm, dry clothes on as soon as you start to feel cold. Take extra food and eat frequently. Keep dry if you can. Camp quickly if you must.

Help a companion who is shivering uncontrollably or seems confused, even if he or she tries to reject aid. You must warm your companion up with proper shelter, with a fire, with hot drinks and with food. You might even use a sleeping bag if you have one, or even use your own body heat to warm them. Don't leave your companion alone because his or her judgment is temporarily gone, and he or she might not survive if you leave for help. If your companion's temperature drops too low, they might even die.

(9) In minor accidents, make every effort to help yourself, or to assist a member of your party, rather than summoning outside help.

## Dealing With Severe Injury

If a major accident occurs, you must get outside help. Determine how to help the injured person immediately. Get the injured person to a safe place and try to determine the extent of their injuries. Give them first aid if needed. Keep an open wound clean. Try to keep the victim warm.

Someone must go for help, either a member of the climbing party or another person nearby. If at all possible, somebody should stay with the injured person. If this is not possible, the injured person should be tied on securely if you are in a spot where they could fall easily or wander away. The person seeking help should travel quickly, but with care. The best place to find help is a ranger station or sheriff's office. Give complete information as to the location of the accident, the condition of the victim, and what aid is required. In many climbing areas, the authorities will call nearby volunteer or official rescue squads. These people have the manpower, equipment, and training to deal with such emergencies.

While waiting for help, keep the victim as comfortable as possible. If the party is large enough, get them a sleeping bag from camp. Provide water and food. Try to keep up his or her morale. It may be a long wait.

## Choosing a Climbing Site

In choosing a climbing site, you may pick out the cliff, peak, or boulder of your choice and attempt to climb it. But most of the time the choice is not that simple. How do you know if the route matches your ability? Are there restrictions on climbing in certain areas? Here is how to find the answers to these questions.

## Climbing Classifications

As soon as your climbing career begins, you will hear about routes classified by class, grade, letter, number, and decimal point. These are symbols used in various climbing classification systems to indicate briefly the length, difficulty, and equipment needed on a given climb. They also provide a basis for comparison between climbs. All such rating systems assume that you are a competent climber. American rating systems refer to routes that are primarily on rock.

### Reasons for Classifying Climbs

Ratings help you choose climbs suitable for your ability or experience. First find out what system is used in your local area. Next, ask climbers and refer to rock climbing guidebooks. Familiarize yourself with the symbols used to describe climbs you have made, and what they mean in terms of climbing difficulty. Compare a familiar system with the one used in a new area.

### The Decimal System

A major system used in the United States and in Canada is the Decimal System (also called the Yosemite Decimal System or YDS). Like other systems, it changes from time to time as the sport of climbing changes.

The Decimal System began with the old Sierra Club System, which also included climber equipment needs. The Decimal System number describes the most difficult pitch of the climb. Beginning and intermediate climbers will be interested in Class 4 and the easier subdivisions of Class 5.

*Class ratings describe the difficult pitch of a route.*

♦ Class 1—Hiking. Any footgear adequate.
♦ Class 2—Proper footgear necessary for rough terrain. Occasional handholds used.
♦ Class 3—Scrambling. Hands may be used frequently. Ropes should be available for occasional use.
♦ Class 4—Ropes and belays must be used continuously for safety. Belay anchors may be necessary.
♦ Class 5—Leader protection required above the belayer. Direct aid must be used.
♦ Class 6—Direct aid must be used.

The class rating describes only the most difficult pitch of a route, which is only one factor to consider when planning a climb. So the Decimal System adds grades in Roman numerals I through VI to indicate the overall difficulty of the technical part of the climb. It also provides an approximation of the time involved to complete the climb. Following are the times assigned to the grades:

♦ Grade I—A few hours
♦ Grade II—Half a day
♦ Grade III—Most of a day
♦ Grade IV—A long day
♦ Grade V—A day and a half to two days
♦ Grade VI—Several days

### Climbing Regulations

In some areas, permission to climb must be obtained beforehand, depending at times on the party's experience. In many places, official permits are required  not only for climbing, but also for camping, hiking, or even for entering a piece of property.

### Private Property

If you want to climb on private property, or in areas reached by crossing private property, ask the owner's permission. Be courteous, explain your activities, and obey any requests the owner may have. Do not damage anything on the property, and carry out all your litter.

### National Parks and Monuments

Many national parks and monuments regulate camping, motor vehicle use, and sometimes climbing. Climbers should register

National parks offer some of the best rock climbing in the world.

before and after climbs. Regulations change frequently. Anyone planning to camp and climb in national parks and monuments should find out in advance about current regulations. Be sure to check with rangers upon your arrival. Rangers can often provide useful information about routes and approaches. They may also offer suggestions for your safety. Signing out for climbs and signing back in are routine. Telephone directory listing for national parks can be found under *United States Government, Interior, Department of.*

### Wilderness Areas

Most wilderness areas and many national forests require permits before climbers and others may enter specific regions. Rules vary from place to place, and from time to time. Restrictions generally cover the total number of users at any one time. They also cover seasonal entry, wildlife refuges, motor vehicles, camping, and open fires.

Before making final arrangements to climb in a specific area, apply for a written permit. The written permit will also contain a list of current regulations from the nearest United States Forest Service office or ranger station. You will find the number listed in the phone book under *United States Government, Agriculture, Department of.*

### Climbing in Foreign Countries

After gaining experience close to home, you may have the opportunity to climb in foreign mountain ranges. There, the climate, rocks, customs, and sources of information will naturally vary. Your first foreign climbs will probably be in Canada.

### Canada

Striking mountain ranges run north-south in the provinces of British Columbia, Alberta, and in the Yukon territory. Many well-known peaks for rock climbing lie within the boundaries of the Banff, the Jasper, and the Glacier national parks.

## Rock Climbing Clubs

Clubs for climbers and clubs for mountaineers abound in the United States and around the world. General outdoor clubs or conservation clubs often have specialized climbing sections. A few large associations include climbing groups. Most colleges and universities, and some high schools, have outing or climbing clubs. These clubs usually offer formal and informal instruction.

Club members usually are volunteers. Charges, if any, usually cover out-of-pocket expenses. Clubs also present programs about climbing.  They also publish a wide variety of newsletters, bulletins, journals, guidebooks, and other informative material.

A list follows of some of the larger clubs that can provide  a great deal of information about various regions.  They often include names of climbing groups in specific areas:

- Adirondack Mountain Club, Inc., 172 Ridge St., Glens Falls, New York.

- American Alpine Club, 113 E. 90th St., New York, New York (no outings).

- Appalachian Mountain Club, 5 Joy St., Boston, Massachusetts.

- Chicago Mountaineering Club, 2901 S. Parkway, Chicago, Illinois.

- Colorado Mountain Club, 2530 W. Alameda Ave., Denver, Colorado.

- Iowa Mountaineers, P. O. Box 163, Iowa City, Iowa.

- Mazamas, 909 N.W. Nineteenth Ave., Portland, Oregon.

- The Mountaineers, 719 Pike St., Seattle, Washington.

- New England Trail Conference, Box 241, Princeton, Massachusetts.

- Potomac Appalachian Trail Club, 1118 N St., N.W., Washington, D.C.

- Sierra Club, 530 Bush St., San Francisco, California (nationwide).

- Wasatch Mountain Club, 425 S. 8th W., Salt Lake City, Utah.

# Bibliography

*Advanced Rockcraft,* by Royal Robbins. La Siesta Press, Glendale, CA. 1973.

*Basic Rockcraft,* by Royal Robbins, La Siesta Press, Glendale, CA. 1971.

*Climbing Ice,* by Yvon Chouinard. Sierra Club Books in association with the American Alpine Club. San Francisco, CA. 1978.

*Icecraft,* by Norman Kingsley. La Siesta Press, Glendale, CA. 1975.

*The Ice Experience,* by Jeff Lowe. Contemporary Books, Inc., Chicago, IL. 1979.

*Learning to Rock Climb,* by Michael Loughman. Sierra Club Books, San Francisco, CA. 1981.

*Mountaineering: The Freedom of the Hills,* Ed Peters, ed. The Mountaineers, Seattle, WA. 4th ed., 1982.

# Glossary

- Belaying—to obtain a hold during rock climbing.

- Bouldering—to climb a boulder.

- Chocks—metal wedges used in rock climbing.

- Carabiners—a metal ring that snaps into the hole in a piton to hold a rope.

- Circumference—the external boundary of an object.

- Diameter—the length of a straight line through the center of an object.

- Elasticity—the capability of a strained object to recover its size and shape after being stretched.

- Foot jams—footholds in the cracks of rocks.

- Hypothermia—subnormal body temperature.

- Pitch—the slope of an object.

- Piton—a spike or wedge that is driven into a rock as a support.

- Rappel—a method of descending steep rocks by sliding down a rope.

- Rucksack—a backpack.

- Swami belt—rope-webbing wound around the waist of a rock climber.